How To Keep Your Kids (and Parents) Safer Online

by John Christly, Carolyn Christly, and Olivia Christly

Table of Contents

About the Authors 3

Some words from John Christly… 4

CHAPTER 1: Navigating the Online World with Your Kids 5

CHAPTER 2: Understanding the Risks of Social Media 9

CHAPTER 3: Recognizing and Avoiding Online Scams 13

CHAPTER 4: The Dangers of Oversharing: Why Kids Should Be Cautious with Their Online Presence 17

CHAPTER 5: The Hidden Perils of Sharing Passwords: A Cautionary Tale for Teens 21

CHAPTER 6: The Selfie Dilemma: Navigating Online with Safety and Respect 24

CHAPTER 7: Navigating the Benefits and Risks of Sharing Your Location 27

CHAPTER 8: Unveiling Catfishing and Impersonation Online 30

CHAPTER 9: Building Trust and Communication with Your Kids 34

CHAPTER 10: Setting Boundaries and Establishing Rules for Online Safety 38

CHAPTER 11: Monitoring and Supervising Your Child's Online Activity 42

CHAPTER 12: Teaching Kids to Think Before They Click 46

CHAPTER 13: Cybersecurity Guidelines for Parents and Senior Citizens 49

CHAPTER 14: Empowering Kids to Report Concerns and Seek Help 56

CHAPTER 15: Reporting Online Scams and Frauds 59

Appendix 62

For the kids – a coloring project... 64

About the Authors

John Christly **Carolyn Christly** **Olivia Christly**

The Christly family (John, Carolyn, and their daughter Olivia) are true visionaries in the world of online security and ways to stay safer online. They each bring unique experiences and advice that can help you and your family navigate the sometimes difficult *(and at times downright scary)* world of online activities.

In "**How to Keep Your Kids (and Parents) Safer Online**," the Christly family delves deep into their combined wealth of experience, offering readers invaluable perspectives garnered from years of real-world experiences and in the case of John Christly, years of serving on the frontlines of corporate cyber defense.

Whether you're a parent trying to learn more about how to keep your kids safer online, or a child of a parent trying to keep your parents safe online, or maybe you are a cybersecurity professional seeking to stay ahead of the curve, this book promises to be an indispensable guide on your journey through the online digital frontier.

Some words from John Christly...

Hello and welcome to our book! We are glad you have found this publication.

Developing this book was truly a labor of love for our family. We are very proud to be able to share it with you. Please share it with your family, friends, and co-workers.

This book would not have been possible without the unwavering support provided by my wife Carolyn and my daughter Olivia. They are the foundations in my life!

Those that know me well know that I am a passionate IT and cybersecurity professional. With a background in military service and a deep understanding of industry regulations, I bring a unique perspective to the IT and cybersecurity landscape.

I have been "in the trenches" for many years now serving in key roles such as CIO, CISO, and CTO, and helping organizations of all sizes to build resilient IT systems, fortify their security systems, and grow security related practice offerings.

I also own my own consulting company and have been fortunate to help many customers over the years with IT security issues that they needed help with.

But when it comes to how best to talk to kids and parents (and especially teens and elderly parents) about how to stay safe in our online world – I knew I could not do this alone, and I would be better off consulting with 2 subject matter experts that I turn to when I have questions about how to teach others how to do things safer online.

And who would be better for me to have provide expert input on this topic besides my wife and my daughter? After all, they are both way more "hip" on certain areas of online culture than I am – and trust me, their expertise and advice can help you too!

I welcome you to connect with me on LinkedIn or check out our company website at **https://omcsystems.com** where you will find links to my podcast series, links to my courses on Udemy, and ways to contact me if you need consulting help.

Thanks again for being here.

I truly hope you enjoy our book.

John Christly, CISSP, CFE, LSSMBB

https://www.linkedin.com/in/johnchristly/

CHAPTER 1:

Navigating the Online World with Your Kids

Welcome to the world of parenting in the digital age! Navigating the online world with your kids can be both exciting and challenging. As a parent, you want to ensure your children are safe and responsible online users. With technology constantly evolving, it's essential to stay informed and proactive in guiding your kids through the digital landscape.

Social media plays a significant role in our lives today, and as parents, it's crucial to understand its impact on our children. From Instagram to TikTok to Snapchat, kids are engaging with these platforms at younger ages, and it's important to have open conversations about the potential risks they may encounter. Discussing topics like cyberbullying, online privacy, and the dangers of interacting with strangers can help empower your children to make smart decisions when using social media.

When it comes to setting boundaries for online safety, consistency is key. Establishing clear rules around screen time, device usage, and the types of websites and apps your kids can access can create a safe and healthy digital environment for your family. By modeling responsible online behavior yourself and enforcing these guidelines consistently, you can help your children develop good habits and make informed choices online.

Open communication is essential in fostering a trusting relationship with your kids when it comes to their online activities. Encourage them to come to you with any concerns or questions they may have about their online experiences. By creating a safe space for dialogue and actively listening to their thoughts and feelings, you can better understand their online world and provide guidance and support when needed.

Staying informed about the latest trends in online safety is crucial for parents looking to protect their children in the digital age. Familiarize yourself with parental control tools, privacy settings on social media platforms, and resources for teaching kids about cybersecurity. Empower yourself with knowledge so you can effectively guide your children in navigating the digital landscape with confidence and security.

Promoting online safety for kids requires a collaborative effort between parents and children. By staying informed, setting boundaries, fostering open communication, and maintaining a proactive approach, you can help your kids develop the skills and awareness they need to navigate the online world safely and responsibly. So, dive into these conversations with your kids, empower them with the tools they need to thrive online, and build a strong foundation for their digital well-being.

CHAPTER 2:

Understanding the Risks of Social Media

Social media, oh boy, don't even get me started on that wild ride. It's like a 24/7 carnival that never sleeps, always buzzing with updates, likes, and comments. But while we're all having a blast sharing our selfies and cat videos, there's a whole other side of social media that we need to be wary of - the privacy pitfall.

Picture this: you're just casually strolling through your feed, liking your friend's vacation pics and sharing hilarious memes left and right. But what you might not realize is that every click, every scroll, every little interaction is leaving a digital breadcrumb trail for data-hungry companies to gobble up. Your location, your interests, your deepest darkest secrets - it's all up for grabs unless you're the Sherlock Holmes of privacy settings, ready to lock down your personal info like a boss.

And let's talk about cyberbullies, those online trolls who lurk in the shadows, ready to pounce on anyone who dares to be different. The cloak of anonymity that social media provides can turn even the nicest folks into keyboard warriors, spewing venom and hate like there's no tomorrow. As a parent, it's crucial to arm your kids with the wisdom and the courage to stand up to these bullies, to report them, and most importantly, to rise above the hate with a heart full of resilience.

But wait, there's more. The glossy facade of perfection that social media presents can be a real head-spinner. The perfectly filtered selfies, the envy-inducing vacation snapshots, the meticulously curated feeds - they can all make us feel like our own lives just don't measure up. It's up to us, the gatekeepers of reality, to remind our kids that true beauty lies in imperfections, and real happiness in being authentic, flaws and all.

And let's not forget the endless scroll, that black hole of digital distraction that can suck us in and spit us out, bleary-eyed and disconnected from the real world. The constant dopamine hits, the FOMO-inducing stories - they can all mess with our heads if we're not careful. So, remind yourself, your friends, your kids - heck, remind everyone

- to find that sweet spot of balance, to unplug and unwind, and to savor the offline moments as much as the online ones.

So, friends, as you wade through the ever-choppy waters of social media, remember this: stay informed and most of all, stay true to yourself. Let your authenticity shine like a guiding star, leading you through the ups and downs of this crazy, digital world we live in.

And hey, don't forget to have some fun along the way - after all, social media isn't all doom and gloom; it's also a place where friendships blossom, creativity thrives, and cat videos reign supreme.

CHAPTER 8: Unveiling Catfishing and Impersonation Online

Furthermore, constantly being under surveillance can lead to feelings of suffocation or invasion of privacy. It's important for teenagers to start to establish boundaries and communicate their comfort levels with location-sharing to their peers and family members. This needs to be done as a compromise with their parents because it involves personal safety issues.

Everyone deserves autonomy over their personal space, even in the digital realm. Teens should have open discussions with their parents about how they feel about having their location shared in apps like Life360, and parents should reassure their kids about why they need to have this service enabled and in use to better protect their kids, not necessarily to spy on where they are.

While sharing your location on apps like Life360 and Snapchat can offer convenience and safety benefits, it's essential to weigh these advantages against the potential risks. Teenagers should approach location-sharing with caution, being mindful of who they share their whereabouts with and regularly reassessing their privacy settings. By staying informed and proactive, you can enjoy the perks of connectedness without compromising your safety and privacy.

In today's digital age, sharing our whereabouts has become as common as sharing a funny meme. Apps like Life360 and Snapchat offer features that allow users to share their real-time location with friends and family. While these tools can provide a sense of security and connection, they also come with potential risks that kids and parents should be aware of before hitting that "share location" button.

Let's start with the benefits. Sharing your location on apps like Life360 can provide peace of mind for both you and your loved ones. Parents often use these apps to keep track of their teenagers' whereabouts, ensuring they arrive safely at their destinations. Likewise, sharing your location with friends on Snapchat can make it easier to coordinate plans and meet up, enhancing social interactions.

Moreover, location-sharing can serve as a safety net in emergencies. If you find yourself in a dangerous situation or get lost, having your location readily available to trusted contacts can expedite in helping to reach you. This feature can be particularly valuable for teenagers who may be navigating unfamiliar environments or staying out late.

However, alongside these benefits, there are important considerations about privacy and safety. Sharing your location indiscriminately can expose you to potential risks. For instance, broadcasting your whereabouts to a large audience on Snapchat could inadvertently reveal sensitive information to strangers or acquaintances. This openness may compromise your safety, especially if you're sharing your location with people you don't entirely trust.

CHAPTER 7:

Navigating the Benefits and Risks of Sharing Your Location

and beauty. It reinforces the notion that one's value is tied to their physical appearance, rather than their talents, intellect, or character.

It's essential for teenagers to prioritize their safety, dignity, and self-respect in the digital realm. Before snapping and sharing a selfie, ask yourself: Am I comfortable with this image being public? Would I want my parents, teachers, or future employers to see it? Am I contributing to a culture of respect and empowerment?

Remember, there are countless ways to express yourself creatively and connect with others online without compromising your integrity or safety. Share selfies that showcase your personality, talents, and interests, while also respecting your boundaries and privacy. By cultivating a mindful approach to selfie culture, you can navigate the digital landscape with confidence and authenticity.

Selfies have become an integral part of teenage culture, serving as a means of self-expression, documentation, and social interaction. However, the trend of sharing selfies online comes with inherent risks, especially when it involves posting images where one is not fully clothed.

It's crucial for teenagers to understand why they need to exercise extreme caution when taking and posting such selfies. First and foremost, sharing revealing selfies online can have serious consequences for your privacy and safety. Once an image is posted online, it's nearly impossible to control who sees it or how it's shared. Even if you trust your friends and followers, there's always the risk of your photos being screenshotted, saved, or circulated without your consent. These images can end up in the wrong hands, potentially leading to harassment, cyberbullying, or even exploitation.

Moreover, posting revealing selfies can have long-term implications for your reputation and future opportunities. Colleges, employers, and even potential romantic partners often scour social media profiles to glean insights into a person's character. Posting inappropriate or provocative photos can send the wrong message and tarnish your online image, impacting your chances of securing scholarships, job offers, or healthy relationships.

Beyond the personal repercussions, sharing revealing selfies perpetuates harmful societal norms and objectification. When teenagers constantly see images that sexualize or commodify the human body, it distorts their perception of self-worth

CHAPTER 6:

The Selfie Dilemma:

Navigating Online with

Safety and Respect

Lastly, sharing passwords can expose you to legal ramifications, especially if the shared account is used for illicit activities. Even if you're not directly involved, being associated with illegal actions conducted under your account can have serious legal consequences and damage your future prospects. Teens need to consider this risk as what they do now may affect them when they are older – often in ways they could not even begin to think about right now.

The dangers of sharing passwords cannot be overstated. As teenagers navigate the complexities of the digital world, it's imperative to prioritize password security and educate oneself about the risks involved. Instead of sharing passwords, opt for secure alternatives like password managers and two-factor authentication to safeguard your online accounts and preserve your privacy and security. Remember, your digital well-being is in your hands.

In today's digital age, where social media, online gaming, and digital platforms are integral parts of daily life, the issue of password security often takes a backseat. It's easy to overlook the significance of safeguarding our digital identities, especially for teenagers who might not fully grasp the potential consequences of sharing passwords with friends or acquaintances. However, the dangers associated with this seemingly innocuous act are real and can have far-reaching implications.

First and foremost, sharing passwords compromises personal security and privacy. Your online accounts contain a treasure trove of sensitive information, ranging from personal messages and photos to financial details. By sharing your passwords, you're essentially handing over the keys to your digital life, leaving yourself vulnerable to identity theft, cyberbullying, and other malicious activities.

Furthermore, sharing passwords can lead to conflicts and betrayals among friends. What may start as a gesture of trust can quickly turn sour if the recipient of your password decides to misuse it or share it with others without your consent. This breach of trust can strain relationships and create rifts that are difficult to mend.

Moreover, sharing passwords violates the terms of service of most online platforms. Many websites explicitly prohibit the sharing of login credentials, and engaging in such behavior can result in the suspension or termination of your account. This not only deprives you of access to the platform but also tarnishes your digital reputation.

CHAPTER 5:

The Hidden Perils of Sharing Passwords: A Cautionary Tale for Teens

safety. And in the end, that balance is what will keep them safe in a world where oversharing is all too easy.

Online predators are always on the prowl, looking for vulnerable targets to exploit. By oversharing personal information, kids are essentially handing these predators the keys to their lives. It's a scary thought, but it's a reality that we can't ignore.

And it's not just about online predators. Oversharing can also come back to bite kids in the future. That embarrassing photo or rant they posted in the heat of the moment? It could resurface years later, haunting them when they least expect it. Once something is out there on the internet, it can be nearly impossible to erase. It's like trying to put toothpaste back in the tube - once it's out, there's no going back.

That's why it's crucial for kids to understand the importance of being mindful of what they share online. It's okay to keep some aspects of their lives private, to hold back on the intimate details that could be used against them. Teaching them about online privacy and safety is not just about protecting them from harm, but also empowering them to take control of their digital footprint.

Having open and honest conversations with kids about the risks of oversharing is key. Encourage them to think before they post, to consider the potential consequences of their actions. Remind them that it's okay to keep some things to themselves, to maintain a level of privacy in an increasingly public world.

By arming kids with the knowledge and awareness to make smart choices online, we can help them navigate the digital landscape with confidence and caution. It's all about striking a balance between sharing and protecting, between authenticity and

In today's world, kids are constantly plugged in, sharing every little detail of their lives online. It's like they're living in a real-life reality show, with their social media profiles serving as their stage. But what they might not realize is that there's a dark side to this constant sharing. Oversharing online can open up a Pandora's box of risks and dangers that can have long-lasting consequences.

Think about it - every photo, status update, or check-in is a piece of the puzzle that makes up your online identity. But what if that puzzle falls into the wrong hands?

CHAPTER 4:

The Dangers of Oversharing: Why Kids Should Be Cautious with Their Online Presence

By staying vigilant, questioning the legitimacy of offers, and being mindful of the information you share, you can significantly reduce your risk of falling for online scams. If you ever feel unsure about something you've encountered online, don't hesitate to seek advice from a trusted source before taking any action. Your online safety is worth the extra caution!

First off, trust your instincts. If something seems too good to be true, it probably is. Scammers often prey on our desire for quick wins or unbelievable deals, so stay cautious when you encounter offers that seem too perfect.

Next, be wary of unsolicited messages or requests. If you receive an unexpected email, text, or social media message asking for money or personal details, proceed with caution. Legitimate organizations typically won't reach out to you out of the blue asking for sensitive information.

Another red flag to watch out for is poor grammar or spelling mistakes in communications. Many scammers operate from overseas and may not have a strong command of the language they're using to target you. So, keep an eye out for any language errors that could signal a scam in the making.

Also, double-check the website URLs you're visiting. Scammers often create fake websites that mimic legitimate ones to steal your information. Before entering any personal details or financial information, ensure that the website address starts with **"https://"** and has a secure padlock symbol in the address bar.

Lastly, never give out your personal information or financial details to anyone you don't trust. Be especially cautious when it comes to sharing details like your social security number, bank account information, or passwords. Remember, it's always better to be safe than sorry when it comes to protecting yourself online.

Catfishing and impersonation online is like diving into a thriller novel, where reality and deception merge into a tangled web of mystery. It's a digital game of smoke and mirrors, where the line between truth and lies blurs, and unsuspecting individuals can find themselves caught in a web of deceit.

Imagine this: you're scrolling through your favorite social media platform, and you stumble upon a profile that immediately catches your eye. The person in the pictures is stunningly attractive, the bio reads like a dream, and the conversations flow effortlessly. You're hooked, drawn in by the allure of this seemingly perfect stranger who appears to tick all the boxes on your wish list.

But here's the kicker - the person behind the screen may not be who they claim to be. Catfishing is the art of constructing a false identity to lure in unsuspecting targets, often to manipulate emotions, extract personal information, or scam individuals. It's a deceptive practice that preys on trust and vulnerability, leaving behind a trail of heartbreak and betrayal.

And then there's impersonation, a more sinister twist in the digital masquerade. This goes beyond merely creating a fake persona; it involves assuming the identity of someone else, using their photos, personal details, and even mimicking their voice or mannerisms. Whether out of malice or simply for the thrill of impersonating another person, the consequences can be far-reaching and damaging.

So, how can you navigate this murky digital landscape and protect yourself from falling victim to catfishing and impersonation? Trust your instincts; if something feels off or too good to be true, it probably is. Don't ignore those nagging doubts or red flags waving in the back of your mind.

There are many things we can do to protect ourselves. Verify their identity; ask for a video call or insist on meeting in person to confirm that the person you're connecting with is indeed who they claim to be. A face-to-face interaction can often reveal more than a thousand text messages ever could.

Do a reverse image search if you suspect someone is using fake photos. Tools like Google's reverse image search can help you determine if those picture-perfect images belong to someone else entirely. It's a quick and easy way to separate fact from fiction in the online world. And most importantly, guard your personal information like it's the key to your kingdom. Never divulge sensitive details or share financial information with someone you've just met online. Your security and well-being should always take precedence over fleeting connections in the digital realm.

In a world where virtual realities can be easily manipulated, it's essential to stay vigilant, trust your instincts, and remember that not everything you see or hear online is always as it seems. Catfishing and impersonation may be the plot twists of the digital age, but by arming yourself with awareness and caution, you can navigate these treacherous waters with wisdom and resilience.

CHAPTER 9:

Building Trust and Communication with Your Kids

In today's digital age, where the online world plays a significant role in our daily lives, it's more important than ever to establish trust and open communication with your children regarding their online activities. Building a strong bond with your kids not only fosters a sense of security and support but also helps you guide them in navigating the complexities of the digital realm.

One of the key components of building trust and communication with your kids is to create a safe space where they feel comfortable sharing their experiences, concerns, and questions about their online interactions. Encourage open dialogue by actively listening to your children without judgment and responding with empathy and understanding. Let them know that they can come to you with any online issues they may encounter without fear of retribution or dismissal. Incorporate discussions about online safety and responsible internet usage into your everyday conversations with your children.

Use real-life examples or news stories to illustrate the potential risks and consequences of inappropriate online behavior. By making these discussions a regular part of your interactions, you are helping your kids develop a critical mindset and a better understanding of the digital landscape. Lead by example by demonstrating responsible internet behavior yourself. Show your children how to protect their personal information, avoid engaging with strangers online, and verify the credibility of the information they come across. By modeling good online habits, you are not only teaching them valuable skills but also building their confidence in seeking your guidance when faced with challenging situations.

Establish clear boundaries and rules regarding online usage within your household. Set age-appropriate guidelines for screen time, social media access, and sharing personal information online. Involve your children in the decision-making process to help them understand the reasoning behind the rules and encourage their active participation in maintaining a safe online environment.

Remember that building trust and communication with your kids is an ongoing process that requires patience, understanding, and mutual respect. Be prepared to adapt and evolve your approach as your children grow and their online experiences change. By nurturing a strong bond with your children and fostering open communication about their online activities, you are equipping them with the skills and confidence to navigate the digital world safely and responsibly.

CHAPTER 10: Setting Boundaries and Establishing Rules for Online Safety

Setting boundaries and establishing rules for online safety is crucial in today's digital age, especially when it comes to our children's well-being. It's a topic that every parent should have on their radar because the online world can be a maze of both wonders and dangers. So, let's dive even deeper and explore how we can ensure our kids navigate this digital landscape safely.

First off, let's talk about setting clear guidelines for internet usage. Think of it like creating a roadmap for your child's online journey - you want to make sure they stay on the right path.

Set limits on screen time and the types of websites and apps they can access. It's all about finding that balance between online exploration and offline activities. And hey, setting some tech-free zones in the house can also help strike a healthy balance. When it comes to personal information, it's like teaching your child to guard their treasures. Remind them not to share sensitive information like their full name, address, or phone number with strangers online. Explain the concept of privacy settings and how they can protect their personal space in the digital world. It's all about instilling a sense of caution and awareness.

Now, let's tackle the tricky topic of online interactions with strangers. It's like navigating a minefield; one wrong move can have serious consequences. Encourage your child to be cautious when chatting with people they haven't met in person. Teach them to trust their gut instincts and remind them that not everyone online is who they claim to be. It's all about fostering a sense of skepticism while still being open to forming genuine connections.

Monitoring your child's online activity is crucial for staying in the loop about their digital footprint. It's like being a backstage manager, ensuring everything runs smoothly. Consider using parental control tools to track their online movements and step in if you notice anything concerning. Remember, it's not about spying on your child but rather about guiding them towards safe online behavior.

By setting boundaries and rules for online safety, you're equipping your child with the tools they need to thrive in the digital world while staying protected. Ultimately, it's about empowering them to make smart choices and navigate the online landscape with confidence. So, keep the conversation going and stay vigilant about your child's online safety - it's a journey worth investing in.

CHAPTER 11: Monitoring and Supervising Your Child's Online Activity

As a parent, it's absolutely essential to be actively engaged in your child's online world. We live in a digital age where screens are a significant part of our lives, and it's crucial to guide our kids in navigating this complex virtual landscape. Having open and honest conversations with your child about their online activities is the cornerstone of keeping them safe and helping them make smart choices.

Setting clear boundaries is like laying down a roadmap for your child's online journey. It's about establishing rules around screen time, guiding them on which websites are safe to explore, and stressing the importance of privacy and security online. Remember, setting boundaries isn't about restricting your child's freedom but providing them with the tools to make responsible decisions.

Parental control tools can be a game-changer when it comes to ensuring your child's online safety. These tools act as a digital safety net, monitoring your child's online behavior, blocking inappropriate content, and even helping you set limits on their screen time. It's like having a virtual guardian angel looking out for your child when you can't be by their side.

Regular check-ins are a simple yet effective way to stay connected with your child's online world. Ask them about their online experiences, the websites they frequent, the people they interact with – it shows that you care and opens up lines of communication. Communication is key in building trust and empowering your child to make smart choices online.

Staying informed about social media platforms and online trends is vital. Understanding the technology your child is using allows you to recognize potential risks and guide them towards safe online practices. The more you know, the better equipped you are to protect your child in the digital realm.

Encouraging your child to share their online worries and concerns is empowering. By being a supportive listener and offering guidance, you help them develop the skills to handle challenging situations online independently. It's about arming them with the knowledge and resilience to navigate the digital world confidently.

Your involvement and guidance play a crucial role in shaping your child's online experiences. By actively engaging with your child's digital life, you are not only fostering a safer online environment but also nurturing a trusting relationship that will benefit them in their digital journey. The key is to be present, supportive, and proactive in guiding your child through the vast digital landscape.

CHAPTER 12:

Teaching Kids to Think

Before They Click

Ah, teaching kids to think before they click - such an essential skill in today's digital world, right? I mean, the internet is like this vast, endless universe where you can find anything and everything, but also where dangers lurk in the shadows. And our little ones are navigating this space every day, so it's up to us to arm them with the tools to navigate it wisely.

Imagine back in our day, there wasn't all this worry about what we clicked on online. But now, with just a tap of a finger, our kids can access a world of information, both good and bad. That's why it's so important for them to pause and think before they dive into the unknown. So, how do we help them with this? It's all about getting them into the habit of questioning and analyzing. Encouraging them to take a moment and consider a few key things before they click can really make a difference. Do they recognize the website or sender? Does the content seem suitable for them? Is there anything sketchy about the link they're about to click on? By prompting them to ask themselves these simple questions, we're helping them build up that critical thinking muscle. They start to realize that not everything online is safe or reliable, and that a little bit of caution can go a long way in protecting them from harm.

And let's not forget about privacy and personal data. By teaching our kids to think before they click, we're also teaching them the importance of safeguarding their information online. They learn to be cautious about who they share their details with and understand how valuable their privacy is in the digital age.

Ultimately, it's about empowering our kids to be savvy and responsible digital citizens. By encouraging them to think before they click, we're arming them with the skills they need to navigate the online world with confidence and awareness. It's like giving them a compass to steer through this digital landscape, so they can enjoy all its wonders while staying safe and secure.

CHAPTER 13:

Cybersecurity Guidelines for Parents and Senior Citizens

In an increasingly digital age, the internet has become an essential part of everyday life. From staying connected with loved ones to accessing valuable information and services, the online world offers a plethora of opportunities. However, along with these benefits come potential risks, particularly for parents and senior citizens who may not be as familiar with technology or its potential pitfalls. Therefore, it's crucial for parents and seniors to stay informed and adopt safe online practices to protect themselves from scams, identity theft, and other cyber threats.

Here are some essential tips to help them navigate the digital world safely:

Educate Yourself: Take the time to learn about the basics of internet safety. Understand common online scams, such as phishing emails, fraudulent websites, and social engineering tactics. Familiarize yourself with privacy settings on social media platforms and other online accounts to control who can see your information.

Use Strong Passwords: Create strong, unique passwords for each online account. Avoid using easily guessable information like birthdays or names of family members. Consider using a password manager (like LastPass, Keeper, and KeePass as a few examples) to securely store and manage your passwords.

Beware of Phishing Attempts: Be cautious when receiving unsolicited emails, messages, or phone calls asking for personal or financial information. Legitimate organizations will never ask for sensitive information via email or text. If in doubt, verify the authenticity of the request by contacting the company directly through their official website or phone number.

Keep Software Updated: Ensure that your computer, smartphone, and other devices have the latest software updates installed. These updates often include security patches that help protect against known vulnerabilities.

Secure Your Devices: Enable security features such as passcodes, PINs, or biometric authentication (e.g., fingerprint or face recognition) on your devices to prevent unauthorized access. Consider installing reputable antivirus and anti-malware software for an added layer of protection.

Be Mindful of Social Media: Be cautious about sharing personal information, photos, or updates on social media platforms. Important: be sure NOT to post your vacation updates while you are still on vacation, as it may signal to others that you are not at home, which they may see as an invitation to break into your vacant house. Adjust privacy settings to limit who can see your posts and profile information. Avoid accepting friend requests or messages from unknown individuals.

Shop Safely Online: Only make online purchases from reputable websites with secure payment methods. Look for *HTTPS encryption and a padlock icon in the address bar* to ensure that your transactions are secure.

Be Skeptical of Unsolicited Offers: If something sounds too good to be true, it probably is. Be wary of unsolicited emails, pop-up ads, or messages promising prizes, lottery winnings, or get-rich-quick schemes. This includes folks reaching out to you asking for you to buy them gift cards or to wire them money. These are often scams designed to steal your money or personal information.

Protect Your Identity: Safeguard your personal and financial information. Avoid sharing sensitive details such as your Social Security number, bank account information, or passwords unless absolutely necessary and only with trusted sources.

Stay Informed: Keep yourself updated on the latest cybersecurity threats and trends. Subscribe to reputable online security newsletters or follow trusted sources on social media for valuable tips and advice. You can also seek advice from friends and family that can help you navigate questions that come up.

Next, let's talk about the "**tech support scam**".

Here's how it typically works:

- Scammers contact you, claiming to be tech support from a well-known company.
- They alert you that your computer is infected with viruses or compromised in some way.
- They offer to fix the issues by remotely accessing your computer.

Once they have remote access, they can:

- Convince you to pay for unnecessary services or software.
- Steal personal and sensitive information.
- Install spyware or other malicious software.

To avoid such scams, remember:

- Legitimate tech support will never initiate unsolicited contact.
- Do not give control of your computer to someone who contacts you out of the blue.

- Do not provide personal information or payment to unsolicited callers or emailers.

If you suspect you've been scammed:

- Update your computer's security software and run a scan.
- Change any passwords that the scammer might have had access to.
- Report the incident to the appropriate authorities.

Always be cautious and verify the identity of anyone who contacts you claiming to offer tech support.

Having a conversation with elderly parents about online safety can be sensitive yet crucial. It's essential to approach the topic with empathy, patience, and understanding of their perspective while effectively conveying the importance of staying safe online. It's important to establish a trusting and respectful environment for the discussion. Begin by expressing your concern for their well-being and reassure them that the conversation is intended to protect them from potential online risks.

To facilitate understanding, it can be helpful to provide real-life examples of online threats such as phishing scams, identity theft, and malware. Use simple language and avoid technical jargon to ensure clarity. Emphasize that just as they would take precautions in the physical world, such as locking doors and being cautious of strangers, similar measures are necessary in the digital realm.

Highlight the importance of strong passwords, avoiding suspicious links and emails, and being cautious with personal information shared online. Encourage them to verify the credibility of websites before making any transactions or providing sensitive information. Offer practical guidance on how to enhance their online security, such as installing antivirus software, enabling two-factor authentication, and regularly updating software and operating systems. Additionally, introduce them to resources and support services available for seniors to learn about online safety, such as workshops, tutorials, and helplines.

Throughout the conversation, maintain a supportive and non-judgmental attitude. Be patient and willing to answer any questions they may have, repeating information if necessary. Encourage open communication and assure them that it's okay to ask for help or clarification. Lastly, reinforce the idea that staying safe online is an ongoing process and that you're available to provide assistance whenever needed. By fostering a collaborative approach to online safety, you can empower your elderly parents to navigate the digital world with confidence and security.

By following these guidelines and staying vigilant, parents and senior citizens can enjoy the benefits of the internet while minimizing the risks. Remember, staying safe online is a shared responsibility, so even if you are not a parent or senior citizen, but you know some, we all can help protect each other. By taking proactive measures, you can help protect yourself and each other from cyber threats and enjoy a (mostly) worry-free online experience.

CHAPTER 14: Empowering Kids to Report Concerns and Seek Help

As parents or caregivers, we've got a pretty important job when it comes to keeping our kiddos safe in this digital age. With everything moving so fast online, it's crucial to make sure our children feel comfortable coming to us with any worries or issues they encounter while surfing the web. We want our kids to know they can always talk to us about anything that makes them feel uncomfortable online. So, have you guys ever come across something weird or unsettling while browsing the internet? It's super important that you let us know about it. We're here to help, and we won't judge you. Your safety is what matters most to us!

Teaching our children the value of speaking up about any strange or unsettling online experiences they may face is key. They need to understand the importance of reporting any inappropriate behavior they come across. Knowing who they can turn to for support, whether it's us, a teacher, or another trusted adult, can make a world of difference in their online safety. We need to show our kids how to use the reporting tools on social media platforms to protect themselves. Whether it's blocking harmful content, reporting cyberbullying, or any other concerning behavior, they should feel empowered to take action to safeguard themselves in the online world.

By encouraging our kids to speak up and seek help when needed, we're giving them the confidence and tools to navigate the digital world responsibly. Your voice matters, and we're always here to listen, support, and protect you. Together, we can create a safer and more positive online environment for everyone.

CHAPTER 15:

Reporting Online

Scams and Frauds

Reporting is crucial to protect yourself and others. Remember, timely reporting helps combat scams and contributes to the recovery of lost funds. Stay vigilant and protect yourself and others from online fraud! Whether you report issue sand concerns to your parents (kids this advice is for you), or to your friends, family, or neighbors – its important to get someone else to help you look into your concerns.

Here are some resources where you can report such incidents:

USA.gov Scam Reporting Tool:

Use the USA.gov scam reporting tool (**https://www.usa.gov/where-report-scams**) to identify a scam and find the appropriate government agency or consumer organization to report it. This tool helps you navigate the reporting process effectively.

Federal Trade Commission (FTC):

If you've experienced a scam, report it to the FTC at **ReportFraud.ftc.gov**. The FTC investigates and takes action against fraud, scams, and bad business practices based on reports from individuals like you.

Anti-Phishing Working Group (APWG):

If you receive a phishing email, forward it to the APWG at **reportphishing@apwg.org**.

For phishing text messages, forward them to SPAM (7726).

Internet Crime Complaint Center (IC3):

If you're a victim of an online or internet-enabled crime, file a report with the IC3 as soon as possible. Visit the IC3 website at **https://www.ic3.gov/** to report incidents related to cybercrime. And last, but certainly not least, you can also report suspicious events to your family, neighbors, and close friends. There is always someone that will be more than happy to help you out.

Appendix

Below are two postcard style contact sheets that you can use to write down names and phone numbers for your family, friends, law enforcement, and others that you would call in case of an urgent issue or potential cybersecurity related scam.

Fill it out, cut it out, and keep it handy in case you need it. Give the other one to friends or family to use.

IMPORTANT CONTACTS

Family and Friends Contacts

_____
_____
_____
_____
_____
_____
_____

Other Important Contacts

USA.gov Scam Reporting Tool
https://www.usa.gov/where-report-scams

Federal Trade Commission (FTC)
ReportFraud.ftc.gov

Anti-Phishing Working Group (APWG)
reportphishing@apwg.org

Internet Crime Complaint Center (IC3)
https://www.ic3.gov/

_____
_____
_____

IMPORTANT CONTACTS

Family and Friends Contacts

_____

_____

_____

_____

_____

_____

_____

Other Important Contacts

USA.gov Scam Reporting Tool
https://www.usa.gov/where-report-scams

Federal Trade Commission (FTC)
ReportFraud.ftc.gov

Anti-Phishing Working Group (APWG)
reportphishing@apwg.org

Internet Crime Complaint Center (IC3)
https://www.ic3.gov/

_____

_____

_____

For the kids – a coloring project

Fido the Cyber Hero Puppy

www.ingramcontent.com/pod-product-compliance
Lightning Source LLC
Chambersburg PA
CBHW030049230526
45471CB00003B/1005